用美国幼儿园课本

学英语

AMERICAN SCHOOL TEXTBOOK

Listening & Speaking Key

step 2

[美] 普特莱克
韩国逸创文化 著

中国纺织出版社

图书在版编目（CIP）数据

用美国幼儿园课本学英语. step 2 /（美）普特莱克，韩国逸创
文化著. —北京：中国纺织出版社，2015.9

ISBN 978-7-5180-1728-7

Ⅰ.①用…　Ⅱ.①普…②韩…　Ⅲ.①英语课-学前教育-教
学参考资料　Ⅳ.①G613.2

中国版本图书馆CIP数据核字（2015）第140926号

原文书名：미국교과서 읽는 리스닝 & 스피킹 Preschool 예비과정 2
原作者名：Michael A. Putlack, e-Creative Contents
Copyright © 2013 by Key Publications
All rights reserved.
Simplified Chinese copyright © 2015 by China Textile & Apparel Press
This Simplified Chinese edition was published by arrangement with Key
Publications through Agency Liang

本书中文简体版经Key Publications授权，由中国纺织出版社独家出
版发行。本书内容未经出版者书面许可，不得以任何方式或任何手段
复制、转载或刊登。
著作权合同登记号：图字：01-2014-5498

策划编辑：张向红　　　**责任编辑：**张向红
责任设计：林昕瑶　　　**责任印制：**储志伟

中国纺织出版社出版发行
地　　址：北京市朝阳区百子湾东里A407号楼
邮政编码：100124
销售电话：010－67004422　传真：010－87155801
http://www.c-textilep.com
E-mail: faxing@c-textilep.com
中国纺织出版社天猫旗舰店
官方微博http://weibo.com/2119887771
北京通天印刷有限责任公司印刷　各地新华书店经销
2015年9月第1版第1次印刷
开　　本：787×1092　1/16　印张：7.25
字　　数：200千字　定价：29.80元

凡购本书，如有缺页、倒页、脱页，由本社图书营销中心调换

American School Textbook
Listening & Speaking Key

Preschool

The Best Preparation for Building Basic Listening and Speaking Skills

The Listening & Speaking Key preschool series is designed to help children, especially preschoolers and kindergarteners, communicate in English. This series helps children develop their listening and speaking skills in a fun and easy way.

Features

- Learning high-frequency words that appear most often in print
- A step-by-step learning process involving the learning of words, sentences, and then questions and answers
- Building basic communication skills and listening comprehension skills
- Exciting topics for preschoolers and kindergarteners that focus on using sight words
- Various activities, including reading, listening, speaking, and writing exercises
- Full-color photographs and illustrations

Table of Contents Vol. 2

Components | Workbook for Daily Review • Answers and Scripts

Syllabus

Unit	Let's Listen	Let's Listen More	Let's Speak
Unit 1 Are You Tall?	**Are you tall?** • Yes, I am. I'm very tall. • No, I'm not. I'm short.	**Is it big?** • Yes, it is. It's very big. • No, it isn't. It's small.	**Is it tall?** • Yes, it is. It's very tall.
Unit 2 Is He Fat?	**Is he fat?** • Yes, he is. He's fat. • No, he isn't. He's thin.	**Who's this?** • It's my father. He's handsome. **Who's this?** • It's my mother. She's beautiful.	**Who's this?** • It's my sister. She's pretty.
Unit 3 Are They Happy?	**Are you sleepy?** • Yes, I'm sleepy. • No, I'm not sleepy. **Are we happy?** • Yes, we're happy. • No, we're not happy.	**Is he hungry?** • Yes, he's hungry. • No, he's not hungry. **Are they cold?** • Yes, they're cold. • No, they're not cold.	**Are you happy?** • No, I'm not happy. I'm sad.
Unit 4 How's the Weather?	**How's the weather?** • It's sunny.	**Is it cold today?** • Yes, it is. / No, it isn't. **Was it cold yesterday?** • Yes, it was. / No, it wasn't.	**How's the weather?** • It's rainy.
Unit 5 Is It Clean or Dirty?	**Is it clean or dirty?** • It's clean. **Is the dog wet or dry?** • It's dry.	**Is he good or bad?** • He's good. **Are they noisy or quiet?** • They're noisy.	**Is it clean or dirty?** • It's clean.
Unit 6 Is It a New Car?	**Is it a new car?** • Yes, it is. It's a new car. • No, it isn't. It's an old car.	**What color is this?** • It's red. It's a red flower. **Do you like red?** • Yes, I do. / No, I don't.	**What's this?** • It's a pencil. It's a red pencil.
Unit 7 Who's Taller?	**Who's taller?** • My sister is taller than my mother.	**Who's faster?** • The rabbit is faster than the turtle. **Is Tom faster than Ann?** • Yes, he is. / No, he isn't.	**Who's taller?** • Jane is taller than Ann.
Unit 8 Who's the Tallest?	**Who's the tallest?** • Mike is the tallest.	**Who's the most handsome?** • Brownie is the most handsome.	**Who's the youngest in your family?** • My sister is the youngest in my family.

Are You Tall?

A Let's Listen

Listen to the Words.

01

a. Listen and **say** the words.

tall   short

strong   weak

b. Listen again and **check** the correct pictures.

1.
☐ ☑

2.
☐ ☐

3.
☐ ☐

4.
☐ ☐

Listen to the Sentences.

a. **Listen** and **say** the sentences.

I'm tall.

I'm short.

I'm strong.

I'm weak.

b. **Listen again** and **number** the correct pictures.

Listen and Speak. Practice the questions and answers.

 **Are you** tall?

1 **Yes, I am.**
I'm very tall.

2 **No, I'm not.**
I'm short.

 Are you strong?

3 **Yes, I am.**
I'm very strong.

4 **No, I'm not.**
I'm weak.

Listen to the Words.

 04

a. Listen and **say** the words.

big   small   fast   slow

b. Listen again and **check** the correct pictures.

1.

2.

3.

4.

Listen to the Sentences.

a. Listen and **say** the sentences.

It's an elephant.
It's big.

It's a mouse.
It's small.

It's a rabbit.
It's fast.

It's a turtle.
It's slow.

b. Listen again and **number** the correct pictures.

Listen and Speak. Practice the questions and answers.

Is it big?

1 Yes, it is.
It's very big.

2 No, it isn't.
It's very small.

Is it fast?

3 Yes, it is.
It's very fast.

4 No, it isn't.
It's very slow.

a. Listen and circle.

1. (a)    b

2. a    b

3. a    b

b. Listen and answer. Then check.

1.    ☐ Yes, it is.
☑ No, it isn't.

2.    ☐ Yes, it is.
☐ No, it isn't.

Is it tall?

Yes, it is.
It's very tall.

Your Turn Ask and answer.

Is it big?
_____

Is it big?
_____

Is it fast?
_____

Is it fast?
_____

A Let's Listen

Listen to the Words. ◉ 09

a. **Listen** and **say** the words.

fat   thin   young   old

b. **Listen again** and **check** the correct pictures.

1.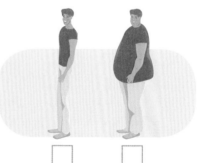

☑ ☐

2.

☐ ☐

3.

☐ ☐

4.

☐ ☐

Listen to the Sentences.

a. Listen and **say** the sentences.

He's fat.

She's thin.

He's young.

She's old.

b. Listen again and **number** the correct pictures.

1

Listen and Speak. Practice the questions and answers.

Is he fat?

① **Yes, he is.** He's fat.

② **No, he isn't.** He's thin.

Is she young?

③ **Yes, she is.** She's young.

④ **No, she isn't.** She's old.

B Let's Listen More

Listen to the Words. ⊙ 12

a. Listen and **say** the words.

pretty   ugly   beautiful   handsome

b. Listen again and **check** the correct pictures.

1.
   ✓ ☐

2.
   ☐ ☐

3.
   ☐ ☐

4.
   ☐ ☐

Listen to the Sentences.

a. Listen and **say** the sentences.

She's pretty.

He's ugly.

She's beautiful.

He's handsome.

b. Listen again and **number** the correct pictures.

Listen and Speak. Practice the questions and answers.

Who's this?

① **It's** my father.
He's handsome.

② **It's** my mother.
She's beautiful.

③ **It's** my sister.
She's pretty.

④ **It's** my brother.
He's handsome.

a. Listen and circle.

1. **a** b

2. a b

3. a b

b. Listen and number the correct pictures.

1

Who's this?

It's my sister.
She's pretty.

Your Turn Ask and answer.

Who's this?

grandmother

father

me

sister

brother

Are They Happy?

A **Let's Listen**

Listen to the Words.

○17

a. **Listen** and **say** the words.

happy   sad   sleepy   tired

b. **Listen again** and **check** the correct pictures.

1.

☑ ☐

2.

☐ ☐

3.

☐ ☐

4.

☐ ☐

Listen to the Sentences.

a. Listen and **say** the sentences.

I'm happy.

You're happy.

We're happy.

I'm sad.

You're sad.

We're sad.

We're sleepy.

We're tired.

b. Listen again and **number** the correct pictures.

1

Listen and Speak. Practice the questions and answers.

Are you sleepy?

1 **Yes, I'm** sleepy.

2 **No, I'm not** sleepy. I'm tired.

Are we happy?

3 **Yes, we're** happy.

4 **No, we're not** happy. We're sad.

Listen to the Words.

a. Listen and **say** the words.

hungry   thirsty   hot   cold

b. Listen again and **check** the correct pictures.

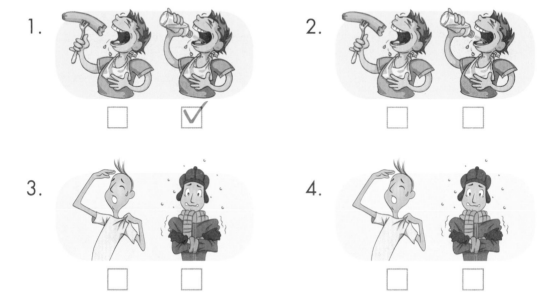

Listen to the Sentences.

a. **Listen** and **say** the sentences.

He's hungry.

She's hungry.

They're hungry.

He's thirsty.

She's thirsty.

They're thirsty.

They're hot.

They're cold.

b. **Listen again** and **number** the correct pictures.

1

Listen and Speak. Practice the questions and answers.

Is he hungry?

1 **Yes, he's** hungry.

2 **No, he's not** hungry.
He's thirsty.

Are they cold?

3 **Yes, they're** cold.

4 **No, they're not** cold.
They're hot.

a. Listen and circle.

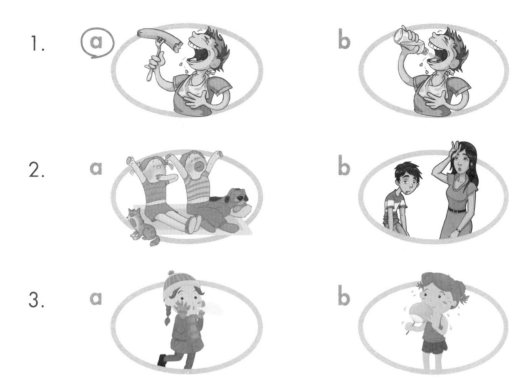

1. ⓐ   b

2. a   b

3. a   b

b. Listen and check the correct pictures.

1.

2.

Are you happy?

No, I'm not happy. I'm sad.

Your Turn Ask and answer.

Are you sleepy?

_____

Are you cold?

_____

Are they hungry?

_____

Are they tired?

_____

How's the Weather?

A Let's Listen

Listen to the Words.

 25

a. Listen and **say** the words.

| sunny | cloudy | windy | rainy | snowy |

b. Listen again and **check** the correct pictures.

1.
   ☑ ☐

2.
   ☐ ☐

3.
   ☐ ☐

4.
   ☐ ☐

Listen to the Sentences.

a. Listen and **say** the sentences.

It's sunny.

It's cloudy.

It's windy.

It's rainy.

It's snowy.

b. Listen again and **number** the correct pictures.

1

Listen and Speak. Practice the questions and answers.

How's the weather?

② **It's** cloudy.

① **It's** sunny.

⑤ **It's** snowy.

③ **It's** windy.

④ **It's** rainy.

Listen to the Words.

a. Listen and **say** the words.

hot   cold   hot and sunny   cloudy and rainy

b. Listen again and **check** the correct pictures.

1.

2.

3.

4.

Listen to the Sentences.

a. **Listen** and **say** the sentences.

Today	Yesterday

 **It's** hot.   ⇨ **It was** hot.

 **It's** cold.   ⇨ **It was** cold.

 **It's** hot and sunny.   ⇨ **It was** hot and sunny.

 **It's** cloudy and rainy.   ⇨ **It was** cloudy and rainy.

b. **Listen again** and **number** the correct pictures.

1

Listen and Speak. Practice the questions and answers.

Is it cold today?

1 Yes, it is.
It's cold today.

2 No, it isn't.
It's **not** cold today.

Was it cold yesterday?

3 Yes, it was.
It **was** cold yesterday.

4 No, it wasn't.
It **was not** cold yesterday.

a. Listen and circle.

1. ⓐ    b

2. a    b

3. a    b

b. Listen and check the correct pictures.

1.

2.

How's the weather?

It's rainy.

Your Turn   Ask and answer.

How's the weather?

A Let's Listen

Listen to the Words.

🔘 33

a. Listen and **say** the words.

clean   dirty

wet   dry

b. Listen again and **check** the correct pictures.

1.
☐ ☑

2.
☐ ☐

3.
☐ ☐

4.
☐ ☐

Listen to the Sentences.

a. Listen and **say** the sentences.

It's clean.

It's dirty.

It's wet.

It's dry.

b. Listen again and **number** the correct pictures.

1

Listen and Speak. Practice the questions and answers.

Is it clean **or** dirty?

① **It's** clean.

② **It's** dirty.

Is the dog wet **or** dry?

③ **It's** dry.

④ **It's** wet.

Listen to the Words.

○ 36

a. **Listen** and **say** the words.

good   bad   noisy   quiet

b. **Listen again** and **check** the correct pictures.

1.   ☑   ☐   2.   ☐   ☐

3.   ☐   ☐   4.   ☐   ☐

Listen to the Sentences.

a. Listen and **say** the sentences.

He's good.

She's bad.

They're noisy.

They're quiet.

b. Listen again and **number** the correct pictures.

Listen and Speak. Practice the questions and answers.

 **Is he** good **or** bad?

❶ **He's** good. ❷ **He's** bad.

 Are they noisy **or** quiet?

❸ **They're** noisy. ❹ **They're** quiet.

a. Listen and circle.

1. a   (b)

2. a   b

3. a   b

b. Listen and number the correct pictures.

Is it clean **or** dirty?

It's clean.

Your Turn Ask and answer.

Is it good or bad?

_____

Is it wet or dry?

_____

Is she noisy or quiet?

_____

Is he clean or dirty?

_____

Unit 6
Is It a New Car?

A Let's Listen

Listen to the Words.

a. **Listen** and **say** the words.

new   old   long short

b. **Listen again** and **check** the correct pictures.

1.
☑ ☐

2.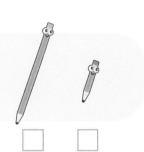
☐ ☐

3.
☐ ☐

4.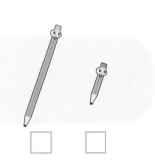
☐ ☐

Listen to the Sentences.

a. Listen and **say** the sentences.

The car is **new**.
It's **a new car**.

The car is **old**.
It's **an old car**.

The pencil is **long**.
It's **a long pencil**.

The pencil is **short**.
It's **a short pencil**.

b. Listen again and **number** the correct pictures.

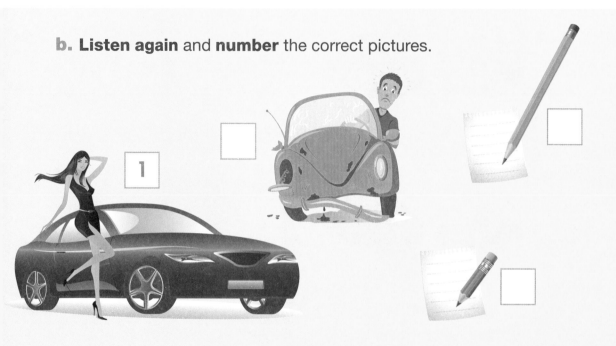

Listen and Speak. Practice the questions and answers.

Is it a new car?

1 Yes, it is.
It's a new car.

2 No, it isn't.
It's an old car.

Is it a long pencil?

3 Yes, it is.
It's a long pencil.

4 No, it isn't.
It's a short pencil.

Listen to the Words.

⊙ 44

a. Listen and **say** the words.

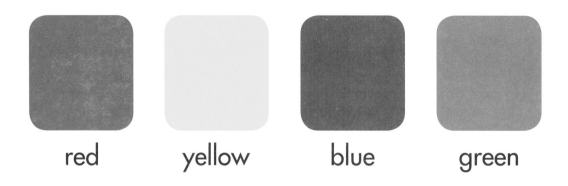

red   yellow   blue   green

b. Listen again and **check** the correct pictures.

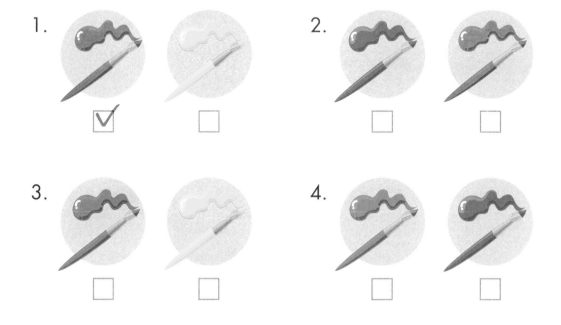

Listen to the Sentences.

a. **Listen** and **say** the sentences.

It's **red**.
It's **a red flower**.

It's **yellow**.
It's **a yellow banana**.

It's **blue**.
It's **a blue balloon**.

It's **green**.
It's **a green cap**.

b. **Listen again** and **number** the correct pictures.

1

Listen and Speak. Practice the questions and answers.

What color is this?

1 It's **red**.
It's **a red flower**.

2 It's **yellow**.
It's **a yellow balloon**.

Do you like red?

4 **No, I don't.**
I like blue.

3 **Yes, I do.**
I like red.

a. Listen and circle.

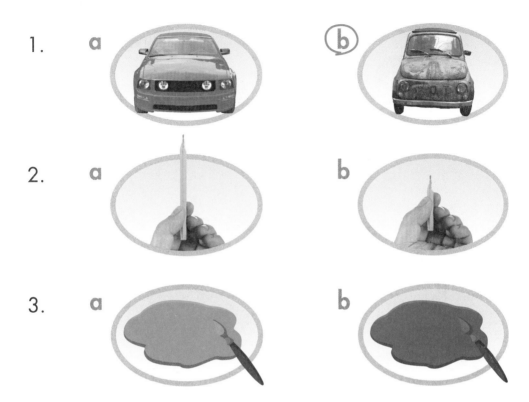

1. a   ⓑ

2. a   b

3. a   b

b. What's this? Listen and number the correct pictures.

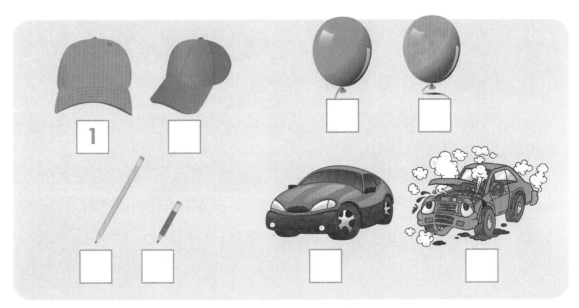

What's this?

It's **a pencil.**
It's **a red pencil.**

Your Turn Ask and answer.

 What's this?

Unit 7 — Who's Taller?

A Let's Listen

Listen to the Words.

○ 49

a. Listen and **say** the words.

tall   taller

short   shorter

young   younger

old   older

b. Listen again and **check** the correct pictures.

1.

☐   ☑

2.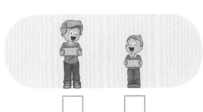

☐   ☐

3.

☐   ☐

4.

☐   ☐

Listen to the Sentences.

a. Listen and **say** the sentences.

The boy **is taller than** the girl.

Jane **is shorter than** Ann.

Tom **is younger than** John.

Lisa **is older than** Anna.

b. Listen again and **number** the correct pictures.

Listen and Speak. Practice the questions and answers.

Who's **taller**?　　　Who's **shorter**?

① My sister **is taller than** my mother.

② My brother **is shorter than** my father.

Who's **older**?　　　Who's **younger**?

me

Jane

Tom

③ My grandmother **is older than** my mother.

④ Jane **is younger than** Tom.

Listen to the Words.

a. Listen and **say** the words.

fast   faster   slow   slower

big   bigger   small   smaller

b. Listen again and **check** the correct pictures.

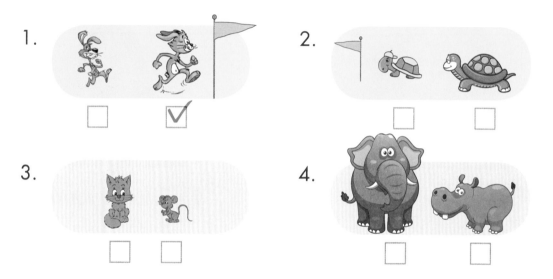

Listen to the Sentences.

a. Listen and **say** the sentences.

The rabbit **is faster than** the turtle.

The turtle **is slower than** the rabbit.

The elephant **is bigger than** the hippo.

The mouse **is smaller than** the cat.

b. Listen again and **number** the correct pictures.

1

Listen and Speak. Practice the questions and answers.

Who's **faster**?

① The rabbit **is faster than** the turtle.

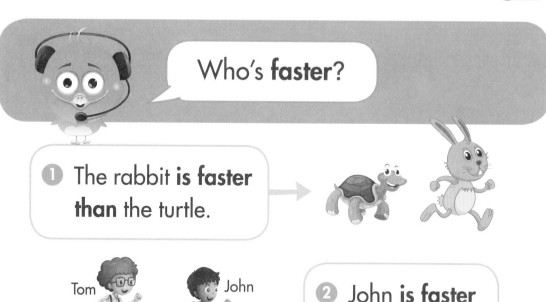

Tom John

② John **is faster than** Tom.

Is Tom faster than Ann?

③ Yes, he is.
He's faster than Ann.

Tom Ann

Ann Tom

④ No, he isn't.
He's slower than Ann.

C Listening Check-up

a. Listen and check the correct pictures.

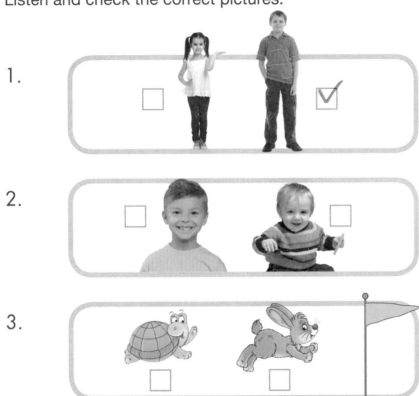

1.

2.

3.

b. Listen and number the correct pictures.

me

1

Who's **taller**?

Jane **is taller than** Ann.

Jane   Ann

Your Turn   Ask and answer.

Who's bigger?

_____

Who's older?

_____

Tom   Ben

Ben   Lisa

Mike   Jack

John   Mina

Who's faster?

_____

Who's shorter?

_____

Unit 8 — Who's the Tallest?

A Let's Listen

Listen to the Words.

○ 57

a. **Listen** and **say** the words.

| tall | taller | tallest |

| short | shorter | shortest |

| fat | fatter | fattest |

| thin | thinner | thinnest |

b. **Listen again** and **number** the correct pictures.

Listen to the Sentences.

a. Listen and **say** the sentences.

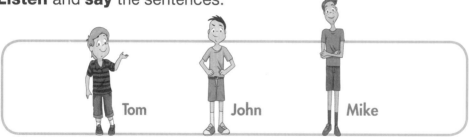

Tom is **tall**.
John is **taller**.
Mike is **the tallest**.

Tom is **thin**.
John is **thinner**.
Mike is **the thinnest**.

Lisa is **short**.
Jane is **shorter**.
Ann is **the shortest**.

Lisa is **fat**.
Jane is **fatter**.
Ann is **the fattest**.

b. Listen again and **number** the correct pictures.

Listen and Speak. Practice the questions and answers.

Who's **the tallest?**  Who's **the shortest?**

1 Mike is **the tallest.** **2** Tom is **the shortest.**

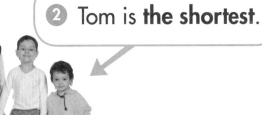

Mike   John   Tom

Who's **the fattest?** Who's **the thinnest?**

Ann   Jane   Lisa

3 Ann is **the fattest.** **4** Lisa is **the thinnest.**

Listen to the Words. 🔘 60

a. Listen and **say** the words.

young   younger   youngest

old   older   oldest

beautiful   more beautiful   most beautiful

handsome   more handsome   most handsome

b. Listen again and **number** the correct pictures.

Listen to the Sentences.

a. Listen and **say** the sentences.

Tom — John — Harry

Tom is **young**.
John is **younger**.
Harry is **the youngest**.

mother — grandmother — grandfather

My mother is **old**.
My grandmother is **older**.
My grandfather is **the oldest**.

Lisa — Jane — me

Lisa is **beautiful**.
Jane is **more beautiful**.
I'm **the most beautiful**.

father — brother — me

My father is **handsome**.
My brother is **more handsome**.
I'm **the most handsome**.

b. Listen again and **number** the correct pictures.

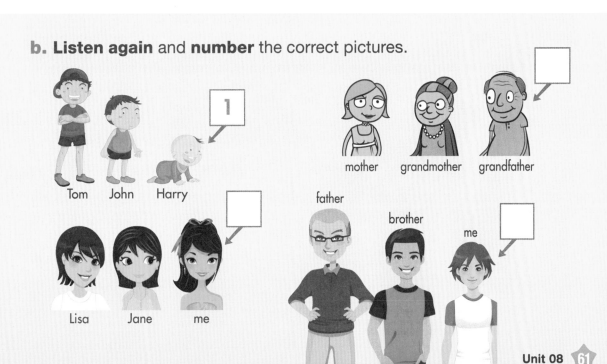

Listen and Speak. Practice the questions and answers.

Who's **the youngest?**

Who's **the oldest?**

① Tom is **the youngest.**

② Jane is **the oldest.**

Tom
age 5

Mike
age 10

Jane
age 12

Who's **the most handsome?**

③ Brownie is **the most handsome.**

Choco

Brownie

Toto

a. Listen and circle.

1. a   b   c

2. a   b   c

3. a   b   c

b. Listen and check the correct pictures.

1.

2.

Who's the youngest in your family?

My sister is the youngest in my family.

me

Your Turn Ask and answer.

Who's the fattest in your family?

_____

Who's the oldest in your family?

_____

me

Who's the most handsome in your family?

_____

Who's the most beautiful in your family?

_____

Word List

Unit 1

Are You Tall?
你个子高吗？

tall	高的
short	短的，矮的
strong	强壮的
weak	弱的
I'm ~ = I am ~	我是……
I'm tall.	我个子高。
Are you ~?	你是……吗？
Yes, I am.	是的，我是。
No, I'm not.	不，我不是。
very	非常
I'm very tall.	我个子非常高。

big	大的
small	小的
fast	快的
slow	慢的
It's ~ = It is ~	它是……
elephant	大象
mouse	老鼠
rabbit	兔子
turtle	乌龟
Is it ~?	它是……吗？
Is it big?	它很大吗？
Yes, it is.	是的，它很大。
No, it isn't.	不，它不大。

Unit 2

Is He Fat?
他胖吗？

fat	胖的
thin	瘦的
young	年轻的
old	老的
He's ~ = He is ~	他是……
She's ~ = She is ~	她是……
Is he ~?	他是……吗？
Is she ~?	她是……吗？
Is he fat?	他胖吗？
Yes, he is.	是的，他胖。
No, he isn't.	不，他不胖。
Is she young?	她年轻吗？
Yes, she is.	是的，她很年轻。
No, she isn't.	不，她不年轻。
pretty	漂亮的
ugly	丑陋的
beautiful	美丽的
handsome	帅的
Who's this?	这是谁？ *Who's = Who is
father	爸爸
mother	妈妈
sister	姐妹
brother	兄弟

It's my father.	这是我爸爸。
grandmother	祖母（外祖母）
grandfather	祖父（外祖父）
me	我（宾格）
It's me.	这是我。

Unit 3

Are They Happy?
他们幸福吗？

happy	开心的
sad	悲伤地
sleepy	困得
tired	累的
You're ~ = You are ~	你是……
You're happy.	你很开心。
We're ~ = We are ~	我们是……
We're happy.	我们很开心。
Are we happy?	我们开心吗？
Yes, we're happy.	是的，我们很开心。
No, we're not happy.	不，我们不开心。
hungry	饿的
thirsty	渴的
hot	热的
cold	冷的
They're ~ = They are ~	他们是……
They're hungry.	他们（很）饿。

Are they cold? 他们很冷吗？

Yes, they're cold. 是的，他们（很）冷。

No, they're not cold. 不，他们不冷。

昨天天冷吗？

Yes, it was. 是的，天冷。

No, it wasn't. 不，天不冷。

How's the Weather?
天气怎么样？

Is It Clean or Dirty?
它是干净的，还是脏的？

sunny	有阳光的
cloudy	有云的，阴天的
windy	有风的
rainy	有雨的
snowy	有雪的

How's the weather? 天气怎么样？
*How's = How is

It's sunny.	阳光灿烂
hot	热的
cold	冷的
hot and sunny	热，有太阳
cloudy and rainy	阴天，有雨
today	今天
yesterday	昨天
It's hot today.	今天（很）热。
It was hot yesterday.	昨天（很）热。

Is it cold today? 今天天冷吗？

Yes, it is. 是的，天冷。

No, it isn't. 不，天不冷。

Was it cold yesterday?

clean	干净的
dirty	脏的
wet	湿的
dry	干的

Is it clean or dirty?
它是干净的，还是脏的？

It's clean.	它是干净的。
good	好的
bad	坏的
noisy	吵的
quiet	安静的

Is he good or bad? 他是好人还是坏人？

He's good. 他是好人。

He's bad. 他是坏人。

Is It a New Car?
它是辆新车吗？

new	新的
old	老的，旧的
long	长的
short	短的
car	汽车
a new car	一辆新车
an old car	一辆旧车
pencil	铅笔
a long pencil	一只长铅笔
a short pencil	一只短铅笔
Is it a new car?	它是辆新车吗？
Yes, it is.	是的，它是。
No, it isn't.	不，它不是。
red	红色的
yellow	黄色的
blue	蓝色的
green	绿色的
flower	花
a red flower	一朵红花
banana	香蕉
a yellow banana	一根黄香蕉
balloon	气球
a blue balloon	一个蓝气球

cap	杯子
a green cap	一个绿杯子
What color is this?	这是什么颜色?
It's red.	它是红色。
It's a red flower.	它是一朵红花。
Do you like red?	你喜欢红色吗?
Yes, I do.	是的，我喜欢。
I like red.	我喜欢红色。
No, I don't.	不，我不喜欢。
What's this?	这是什么? *What's = What is
It's a pencil.	这是一只铅笔。
It's a red pencil.	这是一只红铅笔。

Who's Taller?
谁更高？

tall	高的
taller	更高的
short	短的
shorter	更短的
young	年轻的
younger	更年轻的
old	老的
older	更老的
boy	男孩
girl	女孩

than	比

The boy is taller than the girl.
男孩比女孩高。

Who's taller?	谁更高？
Who's shorter?	谁更矮？
Who's older?	谁年龄更大？
Who's younger?	谁年轻些？
fast	快的
faster	更快的
slow	慢的
slower	更慢的
big	大的
bigger	更大的
small	小的
smaller	更小的
rabbit	兔子
turtle	乌龟
elephant	大象
hippo	河马
mouse	老鼠
cat	猫
Who's faster?	谁快点？
Is Tom faster than Ann?	汤姆比安快吗？
Yes, he is.	是的，他是。
No, he isn't.	不，他不是。

Who's the Tallest?
谁最高？

tall	高的
taller	更高的
tallest	最高的
short	短的
shorter	更短的
shortest	最短的
fat	胖的
fatter	比较胖的
fattest	最胖的
thin	瘦的
thinner	比较瘦的
thinnest	最瘦的
Who's the tallest?	谁是最高的？
Who's the shortest?	谁是最矮的？
Who's the fattest?	谁是最胖的？
Who's the thinnest?	谁是最瘦的？
young	年轻的
younger	较年轻的
youngest	最年轻的
old	老的
older	较老的
oldest	最老的
beautiful	美丽的

more	更加
more beautiful	更美的
most	最
most beautiful	最美的
handsome	帅的
more handsome	较帅的
most handsome	最帅的

Who's the youngest?
谁是最年轻的？

Who's the oldest?
谁是最老的？

age 5	5岁
age 10	10岁
age 12	12岁

Who's the most handsome?
谁是最帅的？

in your family
在你家里

Who's the youngest in your family?
你家里最小的是谁？

My sister is the youngest in my family.
在我家里我妹妹是最小的。

AMERICAN
SCHOOL
TEXTBOOK

用美国幼儿园
课本学英语

Listening &
Speaking
Key

Preschool

学前班篇 2

Workbook | 答案与译文

Are You Tall?

A Listen, write, and match. 🔊 65

1. __tall__
2. _____
3. _____
4. _____
5. _____
6. _____
7. _____
8. _____

| tall | big | small | short |
| strong | weak | slow | fast |

B Ask and answer the questions.

1.

A: Are you strong?

B: Yes, _____. I'm very _____.

2.

A: Are you tall?

B: No, _____. I'm _____.

1. Q: **Is it small?**

☐ ☐

2. Q: **Is it fast?**

☐ ☐

D Listen and number the correct pictures. 67

A Listen, write, and match. 🔘 68

1. __pretty__ .

2. _____ .

3. _____ .

4. _____ .

5. _____ .

6. _____ .

7. _____ .

8. _____ .

fat	thin	young	old
pretty	ugly	handsome	beautiful

B Ask and answer the questions.

1.

A : Is he thin?

B : No, _____. He's _____.

2.

A : Is she pretty?

B : No, _____. She's _____.

C Listen and check the correct pictures. 69

1. Q: **Who's this?**

me ☐   ☐   ☐

2. Q: **Who's this?**

me ☐   ☐   ☐

D Listen and check the correct pictures. 70

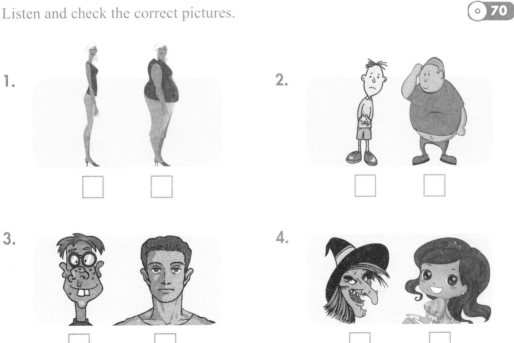

1.   ☐   ☐   2.   ☐   ☐

3.   ☐   ☐   4.   ☐   ☐

Are They Happy?

A Listen, write, and match.

71

1. _happy_

2. _____

3. _____

4. _____

5. _____

6. _____

7. _____

8. _____

sad	happy	sleepy	tired
thirsty	hungry	cold	hot

B Ask and answer the questions.

1.

A : Is she sad?

B : No, _____.

She's _____.

2.

A : Are they hungry?

B : No, _____.

They're _____.

Listen and circle the correct pictures.

1. Q : **Are you tired?**

   a    b    c

2. Q : **Are you cold?**

   a    b    c

D Listen and check the correct pictures.

1.
   ☐   ☐

2.
   ☐   ☐

3.
   ☐   ☐

4.
   ☐   ☐

A Listen, write, and match.

○ 74

1. ___sunny___

2. _____

3. _____

4. _____

5. _____

6. _____

7. _____

8. _____

hot	cloudy	rainy	windy
snowy	sunny	cold	hot and sunny

B Ask and answer the questions.

1.

A: How's the weather?

B: It's _____.

2.

A: Is it rainy today?

B: No, _____.

It's _____ today.

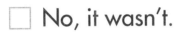 Listen and answer. Then check. 75

1.

☐ Yes, it was.
☐ No, it wasn't.

2.

☐ Yes, it was.
☐ No, it wasn't.

3.

☐ Yes, it was.
☐ No, it wasn't.

D Listen and check the correct pictures. 76

1.

☐   ☐

2.

☐   ☐

3.

☐   ☐

4.

☐   ☐

Is It Clean or Dirty?

A Listen, write, and match. 〇 77

1. clean
2. _____
3. _____
4. _____
5. _____
6. _____
7. _____
8. _____

clean	dirty	dry	wet
noisy	quiet	bad	good

B Ask and answer the questions.

1. A: Is it clean or dirty?

   B: It's _____.

2. A: Is he clean or dirty?

   B: He's _____.

1.

☐ ☐

2.

☐ ☐

3.

☐ ☐

4.

☐ ☐

D Listen and answer. Then write. 79

1.

It's noisy.

2.

3.

_____

4.

_____

A Listen, write, and match.

🔘 80

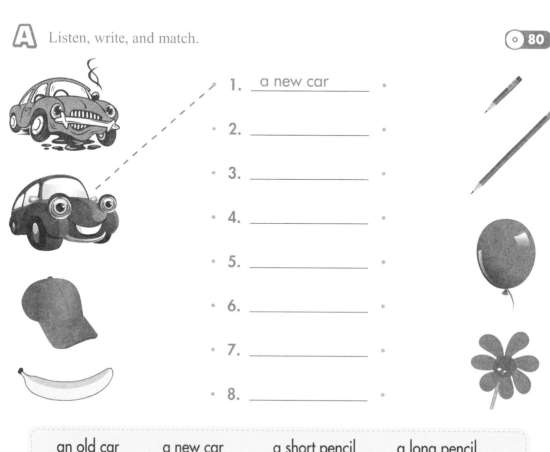

1. __a new car__
2. _____
3. _____
4. _____
5. _____
6. _____
7. _____
8. _____

an old car	a new car	a short pencil	a long pencil
a red flower	a green cap	a blue balloon	a yellow banana

B Ask and answer the questions.

1.

A: Is it a new car?

B: Yes, _____. It's _____.

2.

A: Is it a long pencil?

B: No, _____. It's _____.

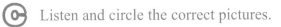 Listen and circle the correct pictures. ⊙ 81

1. Q : **What's this?**

   a 　　b 　　c

2. Q : **What's this?**

   a　　b　　c

D Listen and number the correct pictures. ⊙ 82

85

Who's Taller?

A Listen, write, and match.

● 83

1. taller
2. _____
3. _____
4. _____
5. _____
6. _____
7. _____
8. _____

taller	shorter	older	younger
slower	faster	bigger	smaller

B Ask and answer the questions.

1.
Tom   Ann

A: Is Tom taller than Ann?

B: Yes, _____. He's _____ Ann.

2.

A: Is the turtle faster than the rabbit?

B: No, _____. It's _____ the rabbit.

1.

☐ Yes, she is.
☐ No, she isn't.

2.

Tom

John

☐ Yes, he is.
☐ No, he isn't.

3.

☐ Yes, it is.
☐ No, it isn't.

D Listen and check the correct pictures. ⊙ 85

1.

☐   ☐

2.

☐   ☐

3.

☐   ☐

4.

☐   ☐

Who's the Tallest?

A Listen, write, and match.

🔘 86

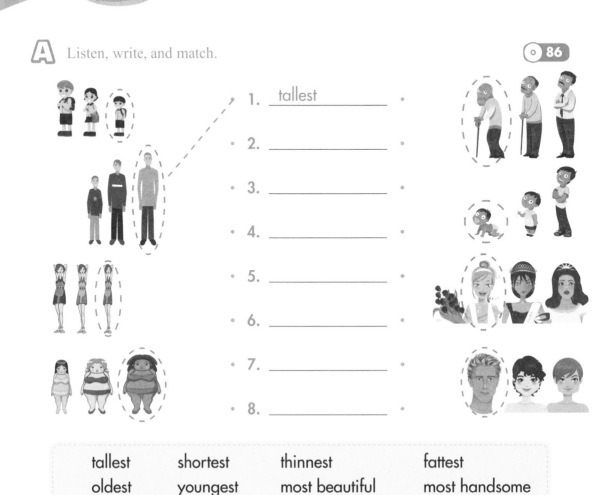

1. __tallest__
2. _____
3. _____
4. _____
5. _____
6. _____
7. _____
8. _____

| tallest | shortest | thinnest | fattest |
| oldest | youngest | most beautiful | most handsome |

B Ask and answer the questions.

1. Mike Tom John

A: Who's the tallest?

B: _____.

2. Mina Jane Ann

A: Who's the shortest?

B: _____.

C Listen and check the correct pictures.   **87**

1.

☐ ☐ ☐

2.

☐ ☐ ☐

3.

☐ ☐ ☐

4.

☐ ☐ ☐

 D Listen and answer. Then write. **88**

1.

brother   mother   father

My brother is the tallest.
_____

2.

Mary   Mina   Ann

_____

3.

Anna   Jane   Lisa

_____

4.

Choco   Brownie   Toto

_____

89

Daily Test 1
Are You Tall?

Ⓐ 1. tall   2. short
3. big   4. small
5. strong   6. weak
7. fast   8. slow

Ⓒ 1. A: Is it small?
   B: No, it isn't. It's very big.
2. A: Is it fast?
   B: No, it isn't. It's very slow.

Ⓓ 1. It's a rabbit. It's very fast.
2. It's a mouse. It's very small.
3. It's an elephant. It's very big.
4. It's a turtle. It's very slow.

Daily Test 2
Is He Fat?

Ⓐ 1. pretty   2. ugly
3. fat   4. thin
5. young   6. old
7. beautiful   8. handsome

Ⓒ 1. A: Who's this?
   B: It's my mother. She's beautiful.
2. A: Who's this?
   B: It's my brother. He's handsome.

Ⓓ 1. Is she fat? – Yes, she is. She's fat.
2. Is he thin? – Yes, he is. He's thin.
3. Is he handsome?
   – No, he isn't. He's ugly.
4. Is she pretty?
   – Yes, she is. She's pretty.

Daily Test 3
Are They Happy?

Ⓐ 1. happy   2. sad
3. hungry   4. thirsty
5. sleepy   6. tired
7. hot   8. cold

Ⓒ 1. A: Are you tired?
   B: No, I'm not tired. I'm hungry.
2. A: Are you cold?
   B: No, I'm not cold. I'm hot.

Ⓓ 1. We're sad. We're not happy.
2. They're tired. They're not hungry.
3. He's thirsty. He's not sleepy.
4. She's cold. She's not hot.

Daily Test 4
How's the Weather?

Ⓐ 1. sunny   2. cloudy
3. windy   4. rainy
5. snowy   6. hot
7. cold   8. hot and sunny

Ⓒ 1. Was it cold yesterday?
2. Was it windy yesterday?
3. Was it snowy yesterday?

Ⓓ 1. It's hot and sunny today.
2. It's windy today.
3. It was cold yesterday.
4. It was cloudy and rainy yesterday.

Is It Clean or Dirty?

Ⓐ 1. clean   2. dirty
   3. good   4. bad
   5. wet   6. dry
   7. noisy   8. quiet

Ⓒ 1. Is the dog dry or wet?
    – It's wet.
   2. Is she good or bad?
    – She's good.
   3. Is she clean or dirty?
    – She's clean.
   4. Are they noisy or quiet?
    – They're noisy.

Ⓓ 1. Is it noisy or quiet?
   2. Is it noisy or quiet?
   3. Is he good or bad?
   4. Is he good or bad?

Is It a New Car?

Ⓐ 1. a new car   2. an old car
   3. a long pencil   4. a short pencil
   5. a red flower   6. a yellow banana
   7. a blue balloon   8. a green cap

Ⓒ 1. A: What's this?
    B: It's a pencil. It's a short pencil.

   2. A: What's this?
    B: It's a flower. It's a red flower.

Ⓓ 1. It's a pencil. It's a long pencil.
   2. It's a car. It's an old car.
   3. It's a cap. It's a new cap.
   4. It's a balloon. It's a new balloon.

Who's Taller?

Ⓐ 1. taller   2. shorter
   3. younger   4. older
   5. bigger   6. smaller
   7. faster   8. slower

Ⓒ 1. Is the girl taller than the boy?
   2. Is Tom faster than John?
   3. Is the elephant bigger than the hippo?

Ⓓ 1. Who's shorter?
   2. Who's younger?
   3. Who's older?
   4. Who's bigger?

Who's the Tallest?

Ⓐ 1. tallest   2. shortest
   3. youngest   4. oldest
   5. fattest   6. thinnest
   7. most beautiful   8. most handsome

Ⓒ 1. Who's the thinnest?
   2. Who's the fattest?
   3. Who's the youngest in your family?
   4. Who's the oldest in your family?

Ⓓ 1. Who's the tallest?
   2. Who's the fattest?
   3. Who's the most beautiful?
   4. Who's the most handsome?

Answers
and
Scripts

答案与译文

Unit 1 — Are You Tall? 你个子高吗?

A Let's Listen 听录音。

Listen to the Words. 听单词。 01

a. 听单词，说一说。

tall 个子高　short 个子矮

strong 强大，强壮，力气大　weak 弱，没力气

b. 再听一遍，标出正确的图画。

Script 1. short　2. tall　3. weak　4. strong

1. ☐ ☑
2. ☑ ☐
3. ☐ ☑
4. ☑ ☐

Unit 01 **7**

Listen to the Sentences. 听句子。 02

a. 听句子，说一说。

I'm tall. 我个子高。
I'm short. 我个子矮。
I'm strong. 我力气大。
I'm weak. 我没力气。

b. 再听一遍，给图片标上正确的序号。

Script 1. I'm tall.　2. I'm short.
3. I'm weak.　4. I'm strong.

1　2　4　3

8 Unit 01

Listen and Speak. 听录音，回答问题。 03
使用下面的提问和回答进行练习。

Are you tall? 你个子高吗?

① **Yes, I am.** I'm very tall. 嗯，是的。我个子高。

② **No, I'm not.** I'm short. 不，不是。我个子矮。

Are you strong? 你力气大吗?

③ **Yes, I am.** 嗯，是的。 I'm very strong. 我力气很大。

④ **No, I'm not.** 不，不是。 I'm weak. 我力气小。

Script 1. Are you tall? – Yes, I am. I'm very tall.
2. Are you tall? – No, I'm not. I'm short.
3. Are you strong? – Yes, I am. I'm very strong.
4. Are you strong? – No, I'm not. I'm weak.

Unit 01 **9**

来，开始试试吗?

B. Let's Listen More 再多听一些。

Listen to the Words. 听单词。 🔈 04

a. 听单词，说一说。

big	small	fast	slow
（身高）高	（身高）矮	快	慢

b. 再听一遍，标出正确的图画。

Script 1. fast   2. slow   3. small   4. big

1. ☑ ☐
2. ☐ ☑
3. ☐ ☑
4. ☑ ☐

10 Unit 01

Listen to the Sentences. 听句子。 🔈 05

a. 听句子，说一说。

It's an elephant. 那是大象。
It's big. 它很大。

It's a mouse. 那是老鼠。
It's small. 它很小。

It's a rabbit. 那是兔子。
It's fast. 它很快。

It's a turtle. 那是乌龟。
It's slow. 它很慢。

b. 再听一遍，给图片标上正确的序号。

Script 1. It's big.   2. It's fast.
3. It's slow.   4. It's small.

Unit 01 11

Listen and Speak. 听录音，回答问题。 🔈 06

使用下面的提问和回答进行练习。

Is it big? 它块头大吗？

❷ **No, it isn't.**
It's very small.
不，不是。
它很小。

❶ **Yes, it is.**
It's very big.
嗯，是的。
它很大。

Is it fast? 它快吗？

❸ **Yes, it is.**
It's very fast.
嗯，是的。
它很快。

❹ **No, it isn't.**
It's very slow.
不，不是。
它很慢。

Script
1. Is it big? – Yes, it is. It's very big.
2. Is it big? – No, it isn't. It's very small.
3. Is it fast? – Yes, it is. It's very fast.
4. Is it fast? – No, it isn't. It's very slow.

12 Unit 01

C. Listening Check-up 听力测验。 🔈 07

a. 听录音，圈出正确答案。

Script

1. Are you tall?
   – Yes, I am. I'm very tall.
   你个子高吗？
   –嗯，是的。我个子很高。   ⓐ   b

2. Are you big?
   – No, I'm not. I'm very small.
   你块头大吗？
   –不，不是。我块头很小。   ⓐ   b

3. Are you strong?
   – Yes, I am. I'm very strong.
   你力气大吗？
   –嗯，是的。我力气很大。   ⓐ   b

b. 听录音回答问题并标出来。 🔈 08

1. **Script** Is it fast? 它快吗？
   ☐ Yes, it is. 嗯，是的。
   ☑ No, it isn't. 不，不是。

2. **Script** Is it small? 它小吗？
   ☐ Yes, it is. 嗯，是的。
   ☑ No, it isn't. 不，不是。

Unit 01 13

---

94 Answers and Scripts

D Let's Speak 说一说。
使用下面的提问和回答进行练习。 08

Is it tall?
它个子高吗？

Yes, it is.
It's very tall.
嗯，是的。
它很高。

Your Turn 轮到小朋友来问一问，答一答了。

Is it big?
– Yes, it is. It's very big.
它块头大吗？
–嗯，是的，它很大。

Is it big?
– No, it isn't. It's very small.
它块头大吗？
–不，不是。它很小。

Is it fast?
– No, it isn't. It's very slow.
它快吗？
–不，不是。它很慢。

Is it fast?
– Yes it is. It's very fast.
它快吗？
–嗯，是的。很快。

14 Unit 01

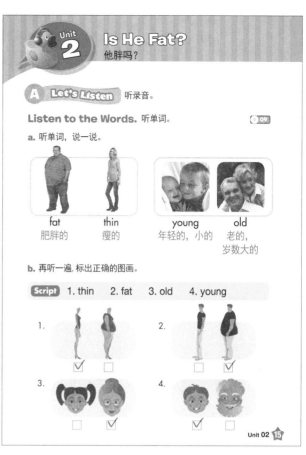

A Let's Listen 听录音。

Listen to the Words. 听单词。 09

a. 听单词，说一说。

fat
肥胖的

thin
瘦的

young
年轻的，小的

old
老的，
岁数大的

b. 再听一遍. 标出正确的图画。

Script 1. thin 2. fat 3. old 4. young

1.　　　　　　　　　2.

3.　　　　　　　　　4.

Unit 02 15

Listen to the Sentences. 听句子。 10

a. 听句子，说一说。

He's fat.
他很胖。

She's thin.
她很瘦。

He's young.
他很小。

She's old.
她年龄很大。

b. 再听一遍，给图片标上正确的序号。

Script 1. He's fat. 2. She's thin.
         3. He's young. 4. She's old.

1　　3　　2　　4

16 Unit 02

Listen and Speak. 听录音，回答问题。 11
使用下面的提问和回答进行练习。

Is he fat? 他胖吗？

❶ Yes, he is.
He's fat.
嗯，是的。
他很胖。

❷ No, he isn't.
He's thin.
不，不是。
他很瘦。

Is she young? 她很年轻吗？

❸ Yes, she is.
She's young.
嗯，是的。
她很年轻。

❹ No, she isn't.
She's old.
不，不是。
她很老。

Script 1. Is he fat? – Yes, he is. He's fat.
        2. Is he fat? – No, he isn't. He's thin.
        3. Is she young? – Yes, she is. She's young.
        4. Is she young? – No, she isn't. She's old.

Unit 02 17

D **Let's Speak** 说一说。
使用下面的提问和回答进行练习。 (24)

> **Are you** happy?
> 你开心吗？

> No, **I'm not** happy.
> I'm sad.
> 不，我不开心。
> 我很伤心。

Your Turn 轮到小朋友来问一问，答一答了。

> **Are you** sleepy?
> – No, **I'm not** sleepy. I'm tired.
> 你困吗？
> -不，我不困。我很累。

> **Are you** cold?
> – No, **I'm not** cold. I'm hot.
> 你冷吗？
> -不，我不冷。我很热。

> **Are they** hungry?
> – No, **they're not** hungry.
> They're thirsty.
> 他们饿吗？
> -不，他们不饿。
> 他们渴。

> **Are they** tired?
> – No, **they're not** tired.
> They're sad.
> 他们累吗？
> -不，他们不累。
> 他们很伤心。

30 Unit 03

A **Let's Listen** 听录音。

Listen to the Words. 听单词。 (25)

a. 听单词，说一说。

sunny	cloudy	windy	rainy	snowy
阳光灿烂的	多云的	多风的	下雨的	下雪的
（天气）晴朗的	（天气）阴天的			

b. 再听一遍，标出正确的图画。

Script 1. sunny   2. windy   3. cloudy   4. rainy

1. ☑ ☐
2. ☐ ☑
3. ☐ ☑
4. ☑ ☐

Unit 04 31

Listen to the Sentences. 听句子。 (26)

a. 听句子，说一说。

It's sunny.	It's cloudy.	It's windy.
天气晴朗。	阴天了。	风很大。
（阳光灿烂。）	（多云的。）	

It's rainy.	It's snowy.
下雨了。	下雪了。

b. 再听一遍，给图片标上正确的序号。

Script 1. It's sunny.   2. It's windy.   3. It's cloudy.
4. It's snowy.   5. It's rainy.

1   3   2

5   4

32 Unit 04

Listen and Speak. 听录音，回答问题。 (27)
使用下面的提问和回答进行练习。

> **How's the weather?** 天气怎么样？

❶ **It's** sunny.
天气晴朗。
（阳光灿烂。）

❷ **It's** cloudy.
阴天。
（多云的。）

❸ **It's** windy.
风很大。

❹ **It's** rainy.
下雨了。

❺ **It's** snowy.
下雪了。

Script
1. How's the weather? – It's sunny.
2. How's the weather? – It's cloudy.
3. How's the weather? – It's windy.
4. How's the weather? – It's rainy.
5. How's the weather? – It's snowy.

Unit 04 33

B **Let's Listen More** 再多听一些。

Listen to the Words. 听单词。

a. 听单词，说一说。

hot	cold	hot and sunny	cloudy and rainy
（天气）热	（天气）冷	热 阳光足	阴天 下雨

b. 再听一遍，标出正确的图画。

Script
1. hot   2. cold
3. hot and sunny   4. cloudy and rainy

Listen to the Sentences. 听句子。

a. 听句子，说一说。

Today 今天	**Yesterday 昨天**
It's hot. 天气很热。	It was hot. 天气很热。
It's cold. 天气很冷。	It was cold. 天气很冷。
It's hot and sunny. 很热，阳光很足。	It was hot and sunny. 很热，阳光很足。
It's cloudy and rainy. 阴天下雨。	It was cloudy and rainy. 阴天下过雨。

b. 再听一遍，给图片标上正确的序号。

Script
1. It's hot today. 今天天气很热。
2. It's cold today. 今天天气很冷。
3. It was cloudy and rainy yesterday. 昨天阴天下雨了。
4. It was hot and sunny yesterday. 昨天很热，阳光很足。

Unit 04 **34** / Unit 04 **35**

Listen and Speak. 听录音，回答问题。
使用下面的提问和回答进行练习。

 Is it cold today? 今天冷吗？

① **Yes, it is.** It's cold today. 嗯，是的。今天很冷。

② **No, it isn't.** It's not cold today. 不，不是。今天不冷。

 Was it cold yesterday? 昨天冷吗？

③ **Yes, it was.** It was cold yesterday. 嗯，是的。昨天很冷。

④ **No, it wasn't.** It was not cold yesterday. 不，不是的。昨天不冷。

Script
1. Is it cold today? – Yes, it is. It's cold today.
2. Is it cold today? – No, it isn't. It's not cold today.
3. Was it cold yesterday? – Yes, it was. It was cold yesterday.
4. Was it cold yesterday? – No, it wasn't. It was not cold yesterday.

 36 Unit 04

C **Listening Check-up** 听力测验。

a. 听录音，圈出正确答案。

Script

1. How's the weather?
 – It's hot and sunny.
 天气怎么样？
 -很热，阳光很足。

2. How's the weather?
 – It's cloudy and rainy.
 天气怎么样？
 -阴天下雨了。

3. How's the weather?
 – It's snowy and cold.
 天气怎么样？
 -下雪了，很冷。

b. 听录音，标出正确的图画。

Script
1. Is it sunny today? – No, it isn't. It's cloudy today.
 今天天气晴朗吗？ -不，不是。今天阴天。
2. Was it rainy yesterday? – No, it wasn't. It was snowy yesterday.
 昨天下雨了吗？ -不，没有。昨天下雪了。

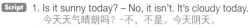

1.   2.

Unit 04 **37**

---

 100 **Answers and Scripts**

D Let's Speak 说一说。
使用下面的提问和回答进行练习。 🔊 32

How's the weather?
天气怎么样？

It's rainy.
下雨了。

Your Turn 轮到小朋友来问一问，答一答了。

How's the weather?
– It's windy.
天气怎么样？
一风很大！

How's the weather?
– It's cloudy.
天气怎么样？
一阴天（多云）。

How's the weather?
– It's cloudy and rainy.
天气怎么样？
一阴天下雨了。

How's the weather?
– It's snowy and cold.
天气怎么样？
一下雪了，很冷。

38 Unit 04

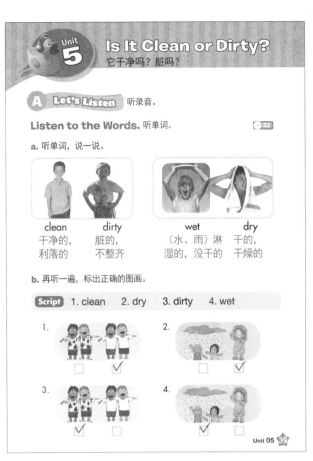

Unit 5 Is It Clean or Dirty?
它干净吗？脏吗？

A Let's Listen 听录音。

Listen to the Words. 听单词。 🔊 33

a. 听单词，说一说。

clean   dirty   wet   dry
干净的，   脏的，   （水、雨）淋   干的，
利落的   不整齐   湿的，没干的   干燥的

b. 再听一遍，标出正确的图画。

Script 1. clean   2. dry   3. dirty   4. wet

1.   2.

3.   4.

Unit 05 39

Listen to the Sentences. 听句子。 🔊 34

a. 听句子，说一说。

It's clean.
它很干净。

It's dirty.
它很脏。

It's wet.
它很湿。

It's dry.
他干了。（不湿）

b. 再听一遍，给图片标上正确的序号。

Script 1. It's clean.   2. It's wet.
        3. It's dirty.   4. It's dry.

1
2
3
4

40 Unit 05

Listen and Speak. 听录音，回答问题。 🔊 35
使用下面的提问和回答进行练习。

Is it clean **or** dirty? 它干净吗？脏吗？

❶ It's clean.
它干净。

❷ It's dirty.
它很脏。

Is the dog wet **or** dry? （下雨了）狗被淋湿了吗？没被淋湿吗？

❸ It's dry.
它没被淋湿。

❹ It's wet.
它被淋湿了。

Script 1. Is it clean or dirty? – It's clean.
        2. Is it clean or dirty? – It's dirty.
        3. Is the dog wet or dry? – It's dry.
        4. Is the dog wet or dry? – It's wet.

Unit 05 41

B Let's Listen More 再多听一些。

Listen to the Words. 听单词。 🔊 36

a. 听单词，说一说。

good	bad	noisy	quiet
好的，善良的	坏的，不好的	吵闹的	安静的

b. 再听一遍，标出正确的图画。

Script 1. good   2. bad   3. quiet   4. noisy

1.   2.

3.   4.

42 Unit 05

Listen to the Sentences. 听句子。 🔊 37

a. 听句子，说一说。

He's good.
他很善良。

She's bad.
她很坏（不好）。

They're noisy.
他们很吵闹。

They're quiet.
他们很安静。

b. 再听一遍，给图片标上正确的序号。

Script 1. He's good.   2. She's bad.
3. They're quiet.   4. They're noisy.

Unit 05 43

Listen and Speak. 听录音，回答问题。 🔊 38
使用下面的提问和回答进行练习。

Is he good **or** bad? 他善良吗？坏吗？

❶ **He's** good.
他善良。

❷ **He's** bad.
他很坏。

Are they noisy **or** quiet? 他们吵闹吗？安静吗？

❸ **They're** noisy.
他们很吵闹。

❹ **They're** quiet.
他们很安静。

Script
1. Is he good or bad? – He's good.
2. Is he good or bad? – He's bad.
3. Are they noisy or quiet? – They're noisy.
4. Are they noisy or quiet? – They're quiet.

44 Unit 05

C Listening Check-up 听力测验。 🔊 39

a. 听录音，圈出正确答案。

Script

1. Is he wet or dry?
   – He's wet.
   他被雨淋湿了吗？没被雨淋湿吗？
   -他被雨淋湿了。
   ⓐ   ⓑ

2. Is it clean or dirty?
   – It's clean.
   那个干净吗？还是乱七八糟的？
   -那个很干净。
   ⓐ   ⓑ

3. Is it noisy or quiet?
   – It's noisy.
   它很吵闹吗？安静吗？
   -它很吵闹。
   ⓐ   ⓑ BARK BARK

b. 听录音，给图片标上正确的序号。

Script 1. They're good. 他们很善良。
2. They're bad.   他们很坏。
3. They're noisy. 他们很吵闹。
4. They're quiet. 他们很安静。

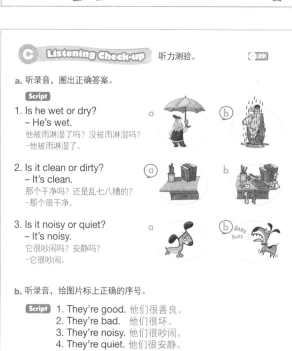

Unit 05 45

---

102 Answers and Scripts

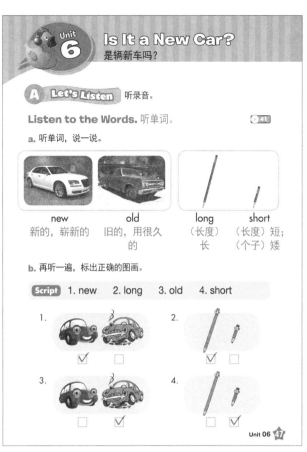

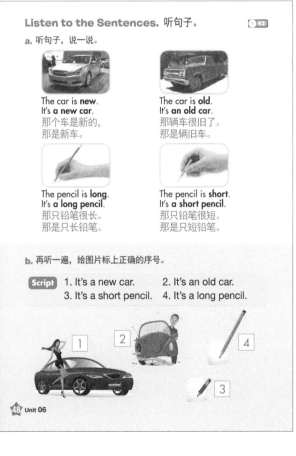

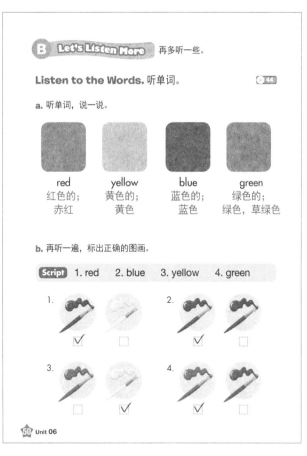

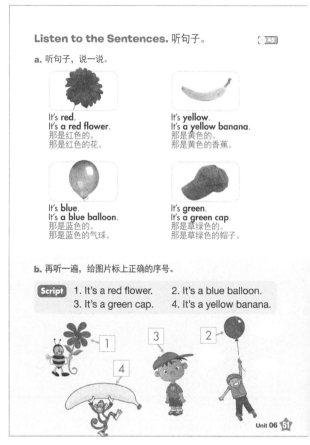

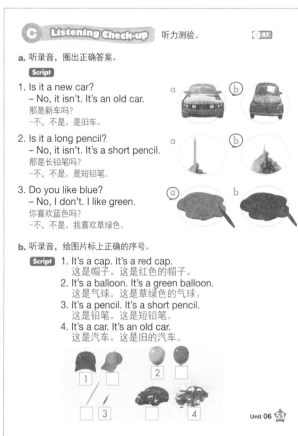

D Let's Speak

说一说。使用下面的提问和回答进行练习。 🔊48

What's this?
这是什么？

It's a pencil.
It's a red pencil.
这是铅笔。
红色的铅笔。

Your Turn 轮到小朋友来问一问，答一答了。

What's this?
– It's a cap. It's a yellow cap.
这是什么？
–这是帽子。黄色的帽子。

What's this?
– It's a car. It's a blue car.
这是什么？
–这是汽车。蓝色的汽车。

What's this?
– It's a balloon. It's a green balloon.
这是什么？
–这是气球。草绿色的气球。

What's this?
– It's a flower. It's a red flower.
这是什么？
–这是花。红色的花。

54 Unit 06

Unit 7 Who's Taller?
谁更高？

A Let's Listen 听录音。

Listen to the Words. 听单词。 🔊49

a. 听单词，说一说。

tall taller
（个子）高 更高

short shorter
（个子）矮 更矮

young younger
年少的，年轻的 更年少的，更年轻的

old older
老的，岁数大的 更老的，岁数更大的

b. 再听一遍，标出正确的图画。

Script 1. taller 2. shorter 3. older 4. younger

1. 2.
3. 4.

Unit 07 **55**

Listen to the Sentences. 听句子。 🔊30

a. 听句子，说一说。

The boy **is taller than** the girl.
男孩比女孩子高。

Jane **is shorter than** Ann.
简比安矮。

Tom **is younger than** John.
汤姆比约翰小。

Lisa **is older than** Anna.
莉莎比安娜老。

b. 再听一遍，给图片标上正确的序号。

Script 1. The boy is taller than the girl. 2. Lisa is older than Anna.
3. Tom is younger than John. 4. Jane is shorter than Ann.

56 Unit 07

Listen and Speak. 听录音，回答问题。 🔊31
使用下面的提问和回答进行练习。

Who's taller?
谁更高？

Who's shorter?
谁更矮？

❶ My sister **is taller than** my mother.
我姐姐比我妈妈高。

❷ My brother **is shorter than** my father.
我哥哥比我爸爸矮。

Who's older?
谁更老？

Who's younger?
谁更年轻？

❸ My grandmother **is older than** my mother.
我奶奶比我妈妈老。

❹ Jane **is younger than** Tom.
简比汤姆年轻。

Script 1. Who's taller? – My sister is taller than my mother.
2. Who's shorter? – My brother is shorter than my father.
3. Who's older? – My grandmother is older than my mother.
4. Who's younger? – Jane is younger than Tom.

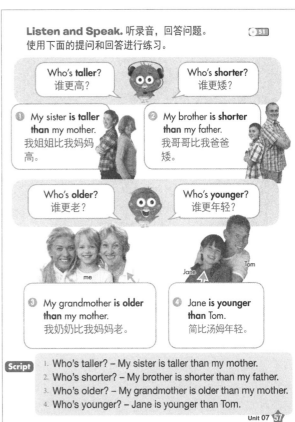

Unit 07 **57**

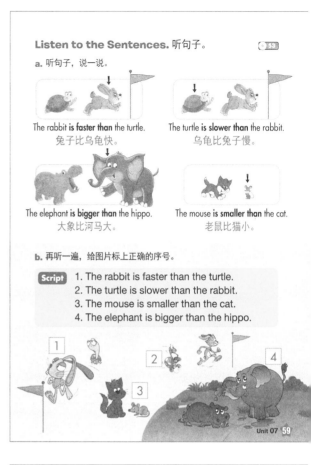

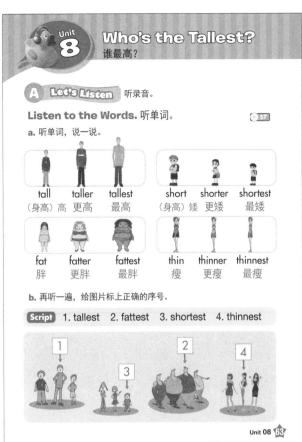

B Let's Listen More 再多听一些。

Listen to the Words. 听单词。 🔊 60

a. 听单词，说一说。

young 年少，年轻
younger 更年少，更年轻
youngest 最年少，最年轻
old 老，岁数大
older 更老，岁数更大
oldest 最老，岁数最大
beautiful 美丽
more beautiful 更美丽
most beautiful 最美丽
handsome 帅
more handsome 更帅
most handsome 最帅

b. 再听一遍，给图片标上正确的序号。

Script 1. youngest 2. oldest
3. most handsome 4. most beautiful

Listen to the Sentences. 听句子。 🔊 61

a. 听句子，说一说。

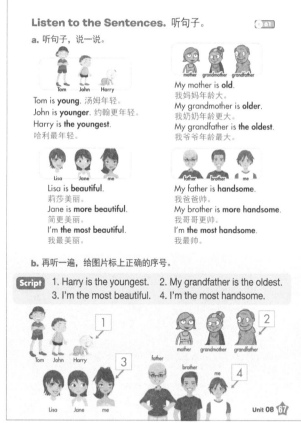

Tom is **young**. 汤姆年轻。
John is **younger**. 约翰更年轻。
Harry is **the youngest**. 哈利最年轻。

My mother is **old**. 我妈妈年龄大。
My grandmother is **older**. 我奶奶年龄更大。
My grandfather is **the oldest**. 我爷爷年龄最大。

Lisa is **beautiful**. 莉莎美丽。
Jane is **more beautiful**. 简更美丽。
I'm **the most beautiful**. 我最美丽。

My father is **handsome**. 我爸帅。
My brother is **more handsome**. 我哥哥更帅。
I'm **the most handsome**. 我最帅。

b. 再听一遍，给图片标上正确的序号。

Script 1. Harry is the youngest. 2. My grandfather is the oldest.
3. I'm the most beautiful. 4. I'm the most handsome.

Listen and Speak. 听录音，回答问题。 🔊 62
使用下面的提问和回答进行练习。

Who's **the youngest**? 谁最年轻？
Who's **the oldest**? 谁年龄最大？

❶ Tom is **the youngest**. 汤姆最年轻。
❷ Jane is **the oldest**. 简年龄最大。

Tom age 5 Mike age 10 Jane age 12

Who's **the most handsome**? 谁最帅？

❸ Brownie is **the most handsome**. 布朗尼最帅。

Choco Brownie Toto

Script
1. Who's the youngest? – Tom is the youngest.
2. Who's the oldest? – Jane is the oldest.
3. Who's the most handsome? – Brownie is the most handsome.

C Listening Check-up 听力测验。 🔊 63

a. 听录音，圈出正确答案。

Script

1. Who's the fattest? 谁最胖？ a b ⓒ
2. Who's the thinnest? 谁最瘦？ ⓐ b c
3. Who's the tallest? 谁个子最高？ a b ⓒ

b. 听录音，标出正确的图画。

Script 1. This is Jane. She's the most beautiful. 这个人是简。她最美丽。
2. This is Mina. She's the shortest. 这个人是美娜。她最矮。

1.
2.